Scotland Panorama

Colin Baxter

Colin Baxter Photography, Grantown-on-Spey, Scotland

Scotland Panorama

Scotland's distinctive landscapes are endlessly transformed throughout the seasons by ever-changing light. Here at Ardban in Wester Ross, with distant Raasay and Skye beyond, the Highlands and Islands beckon.

Scotland Panorama

There is a saying: 'Scotland is the best small country in the world'. Well, it may be small, but Scotland is a land blessed with stunning panoramas sufficient for a whole continent. From the lonely valley of Liddesdale, hard by the border with England, to the remote rocky islet of Muckle Flugga, at the northernmost tip of far-off Shetland, the traveller encounters at almost every turn panoramas that simply compel one to stop, draw breath – then gaze in admiration, and awe, at the spectacle spread out before them.

Scotland embraces just 30,000 square miles and reaches only to a height of 4408 ft (1344 m) above sea-level, and yet it is a land of extraordinary richness and infinite variety. The awesome forces of creation have, over the eons of time, bequeathed a beguiling array of mountains and moors, lochs and islands, rivers and glens. Individually they have the power to impress: the still waters of Loch Garten, Staffa's incredible natural architecture, Tràigh Seilebost's cream-white sands, Buachaille Etive Mòr's grim countenance – and, towering over everything Ben Nevis, Scotland's highest mountain.

But as impressive as these works of creation are individually, it is the manner in which they interact with their surroundings that simply overwhelms us, humbles us even.

In Loch Garten's peaceful waters are reflected the foothills of the Cairngorm Mountains, a fragile paradise of sub-Arctic flora and fauna. Staffa is surrounded by innumerable Hebridean islands, each with a character, a uniqueness, all of its own. Tràigh Seilebost's beach inter-plays with the sweet green machair behind, spangled with wild flowers, and the turquoise seas below. Buachaille Etive Mòr is the gate-keeper at the entrance down into dark, forbidding Glencoe, with its array of towering peaks. And mighty Ben Nevis is the clan chief of 284 'Munros' (the mountains over 3000 ft / 914.4 m) that inhabit the landscape of Scotland, many of which are only known by their original Gaelic names.

No one part of Scotland is quite like another. The Western and Northern Isles are both distant Scottish island groups, but their respective geologies and locations have combined to produce very different archipelagos. The long island chain of the Outer Hebrides, formed from the oldest rocks in the British Isles and lashed by the Atlantic's fierce storms, has a gnarled and grizzled countenance, its peat-bogged interior alleviated at the edges by wonderful sandy beaches and tempting blue-green seas. The numerous islands of Orkney and Shetland, on the other hand, have a greener and more

LOCH TUMMEL AND SCHIEHALLION FROM 'QUEEN'S VIEW', PERTHSHIRE.

fertile appearance, due to their more productive soils. Whilst the Western Isles struggle to sustain life, their northern counterparts have done so proficiently for thousands of years; their wealth of Stone-Age monuments testifies to that.

Variety is evident across the Highlands too. While the mountains of Scotland may give the overall impression of being universally grand, they too have conspicuous differences. Whereas the peaks of the North-West Highlands – Foinaven, Suilven and the rest – are lonely creatures, shunning the company of others, the lofty 'Munros' of the West Highlands group together, most formidably in Lochaber and the Cuillins on Skye. To their east, in the Central Highlands, Cairn Gorm and its neighbours slowly cast off their snowy mantles, whilst the brown hills of Argyll are more rugged than mountainous.

The Southern Uplands south of Glasgow and Edinburgh provide a lowland contrast to these mountain massifs, rolling as they do across the landscape, their gently undulating slopes carpeted in a tangle of heather, whin and bracken. Nowhere do they aspire to the pinnacles of the Highlands.

It is not just Scotland's mountains that offer richness and variety; so also do its waters. Sir Walter Scott described Caledonia as the 'land of the mountain and the flood', and the images in this collection reveal just how central water is in the beauty of Scotland's creation. A handful of broad firths penetrate deep into the fertile plains of the east coast, whilst the rugged western seaboard is shredded by a host of sinuous lochs. Inland lie innumerable freshwater lochs fringed by woodland.

In this natural world the hand of man is understandably muted. In the Highlands and Islands fishing villages cling to the coast like barnacles to a boat, whilst in the straths and glens isolated whitewashed crofts provide evidence of the resilience of the people who work the land. Here too lie the ancient strongholds of medieval clan chiefs and warlords.

It is in the Lowlands of Scotland and up along the east coast that mankind truly comes into its own. Here the enduring impression is of a land of neat, patchwork-quilt fields and, on the slopes above, lush green pastures where cattle and sheep may safely graze. Once formidable castles, and graceful abbeys, remind us of a bygone age. But it is the present-day that prevails in these Lowland panoramas, with bustling fishing ports, thriving towns, and the vibrant cities of Aberdeen, Dundee, Glasgow, Inverness, Perth, and the nation's capital, Edinburgh.

Scotland's rich and varied landscape is out there awaiting the inquisitive traveller. It is here too in this book, captured by Scotland's most prolific landscape photographer.

THE FIVE SISTERS OF KINTAIL AND LOCH DUICH, WEST HIGHLANDS.

The West Highlands and Islands

Mountains and long sinuous sea lochs dominate the panoramas of the West Highlands and Islands.
Here the traveller finds untamed and often remote landscapes, inhabited by snow-capped peaks in winter.
Lurking deep in their shadows lie cool, peat-blackened lochs. Along the deeply indented Atlantic seaboard bask
mysterious Hebridean islands, chief among them Skye, with its majestic Cuillin Hills. The presence of man
is still in evidence among even the more remote areas here – in ancient castles and isolated crofts.

LOCH SHIEL AND THE GLENFINNAN MONUMENT, LOCHABER (left) and BEN NEVIS (above).

URQUHART CASTLE AND LOCH NESS.

For over 500 years great lords held sway from this once-formidable medieval stronghold beside Loch Ness.

GLEN AFFRIC AND LOCH AFFRIC.
Glen Affric – one of the most beautiful of all Highland glens – is hidden away in the
mountains between Loch Ness and the snow-capped peaks of Kintail that rise to the west.

LOCH TORRIDON, WESTER ROSS.
Looking out from the summit of Beinn Alligin (above), the traveller stares into the abyss of time,
for the mountains around Loch Torridon and Loch Damh (right) are over 1000 million years old.

PLOCKTON AND LOCH CARRON, WESTER ROSS.

LOCH SHIELDAIG, TORRIDON, WESTER ROSS.

THE KINTAIL MOUNTAINS AND LOCH DUICH.

EILEAN DONAN CASTLE, LOCH DUICH.
The mountainous land around Loch Duich was 'Mackenzie country' in the Middle Ages, controlled from forbidding
Eilean Donan ('St Donan's Isle'). The castle, blown up during the 1719 Jacobite Rising, was restored in the early 20th century.

THE SKYE BRIDGE AND LOCH ALSH.

THE RED CUILLIN ACROSS BROADFORD BAY, ISLE OF SKYE.
The rounded granite peaks of the Red Cuillin, among them Beinn na Caillach, Beinn Dearg Mhòr
and Glas Bheinn Mhòr, form a formidable barrier across the south end of the Isle of Skye.

THE STORR, OLD MAN OF STORR AND LOCH FADA (left) and THE QUIRAING (above), TROTTERNISH, ISLE OF SKYE.
The Trotternish peninsula hosts some of the most spectacular screes, crags and rock pinnacles in the British Isles.

ORONSAY AND WIAY ACROSS LOCH BRACADALE, ISLE OF SKYE.

Loch Bracadale opens westwards into the Sea of the Hebrides, guarded by islands and basalt cliffs sculpted into caves.

EIGG, RÙM AND THE POINT OF SLEAT, ISLE OF SKYE.

THE CUILLIN HILLS, ISLE OF SKYE – ACROSS LOCH SCAVAIG (left) and INNER SOUND (above).
The spectacular Cuillin Hills dominate the Isle of Skye, drawing climbers from all over the world. Sir Walter Scott,
who visited in 1814, told of 'a scene so rude, so wild as this, yet so sublime in barrenness.' Perfect.

THE ISLE OF RÙM AT DAWN.
Rùm is the largest of 'The Small Isles' (Rùm, Muck, Eigg and Canna) off Skye's south coast. Formerly a sporting estate, the island is now a National Nature Reserve and an important place for ecological research.

BÀGH A' GHALLANAICH, ISLE OF MUCK, WITH RÙM AND SKYE BEYOND.

The Isle of Muck derives from the Gaelic, *eilean nam muc* 'isle of pigs', but cattle now pasture this low-lying island.

ARDNAMURCHAN FROM THE SOUTH.
The Point of Ardnamurchan (far left) is the most westerly point of the British mainland.

ARISAIG, LOCHABER.

The small village of Arisaig lies on the rugged Morar coastline along the 'Road to the Isles'. The island of Eigg rises up beyond.

LOCH MORAR, THE SOUND OF SLEAT AND ISLAND OF EIGG.

BARRISDALE BAY, LOCH HOURN AND THE MOUNTAINS OF LOCHABER (right).

GLENFINNAN VIADUCT, LOCHABER.

The splendidly curved 21-arched viaduct was completed in 1901. It still serves the West Highland Line between Fort William and Mallaig.

BEN NEVIS AND AONACH BEAG FROM AN GARBHANACH, MAMORES (right).

Ben Nevis, on the left, is Britain's highest mountain at 4408 ft (1344 m). Nicknamed 'The Ben', it is climbed some 100,000 times each year.

CHNO DEARG ACROSS LOCH LAGGAN, BADENOCH.

LOCHAN NA E-EARBA, BADENOCH (left).

BUACHAILLE ETIVE MÒR, GLENCOE.

'The great herdsman of Etive', standing sentinel over the upper entrance into the Pass of Glencoe, looks forbidding at any time of the year. The novelist Neil Munro described Glencoe as 'forgotten of heaven and unfriendly to man.'

'THE THREE SISTERS', GLENCOE.

THE PAP OF GLENCOE AND SGORR NAM FIANNAIDH, GLENCOE, ACROSS LOCH LEVEN (right).

Glencoe is infamous for the massacre of 1692, when members of the MacDonald clan were betrayed and murdered by their guests.

Argyll and the Isles

Argyll is a complex pattern of island, sea and mountain. Here the coastline reigns supreme, sometimes straight and stern, as in Loch Fyne, but mostly twisting and turning this way and that, often entwined by rocky coves and little inlets. Offshore a myriad of islands emerge from the waves, among them Mull, Islay, Jura, Coll, Tiree and Colonsay. The sea not only dominates the panoramas, it dominates human life also. Passenger ferries crisscross Argyll's waters and leisure boats anchor in its many harbours.

BEN CRUACHAN AND LOCH ETIVE (left) and OBAN HARBOUR (above).

CASTLE STALKER, APPIN, WITH LISMORE BEYOND.

LISMORE, APPIN AND BENDERLOCH (left).

BREACHACHA CASTLE (above) and TRÀIGH GHARIBH (right), ISLE OF COLL.

The residents of low-lying Coll in former times included the Macleans who ruled from Breachacha Castle.

BALEPHUIL BAY (left) and SANDAIG CROFT HOUSE (above), TIREE.
Tiree lies 22 miles (35 km) off the western shores of Ardnamurchan, and is so low-lying that it is often called 'the land beneath the waves'.
The island is bathed by the warm waters of the Gulf Stream, and its sandy soils sustain a thriving crofting community.

THE ROSS OF MULL AND ARDMEANACH, ISLE OF MULL, FROM IONA (above) and IONA ABBEY (right).
The near-vertical cliffs on the Ardmeanach peninsula contrast with the low-lying green machair of Iona. The monastery of Iona Abbey was founded by Saint Columba in AD 653 and is thought to be the place of origin from where Christianity spread throughout Scotland.

DUART CASTLE, ISLE OF MULL.

The chiefs of Clan Maclean have been holding sway from this formidable fortress for over 800 years.

STAFFA.

The Vikings named it *stafi-øy*, 'pillar island' after the columns of cooled lava formed 65 million years ago.
The colonnade at this south end has pillars reaching 56 ft (17m) high, and the world-famous Fingal's Cave (to the right)
was the inspiration for Felix Mendelssohn's *Hebrides Overture* composed in 1830.

TOBERMORY, ISLE OF MULL.

Tobermory (*tobar Mhoire*, 'Mary's Well') has one of Scotland's prettiest harbours. It was founded as a fishing port in 1788 and constructed to a design by Thomas Telford. The village's Main Street hugs the shoreline, facing out into the Sound of Mull.

BEN MORE AND LOCH SCRIDAIN, ISLE OF MULL.

Ben More is a remnant volcano, and at 3165 ft (966 m) high, the only Munro found on an island, apart from the Cuillin Hills of Skye.

LOCH NA KEAL, ULVA AND EORSA FROM THE SLOPES OF BEN MORE, ISLE OF MULL.

KILORAN BAY, COLONSAY (right).

LOCH GRUINART, ISLAY.

Islay is sometimes referred to as the 'Queen of the Hebrides', and is justly reknowned for its bird-watching and fine malt whisky.

THE PAPS OF JURA ACROSS THE SOUND OF ISLAY.
The steep-sided quartzite mountains known as the Paps of Jura are among the most prominent landmarks in the Hebrides.
Pictured here are Beinn an Oir ('mountain of gold') and Beinn Shiantaidh ('holy mountain').

TARBERT HARBOUR, KINTYRE.

Colourful fishing boats crowd the harbour, where once intimidating warships anchored in the shadow of the royal castle.

THE MULL OF KINTYRE ACROSS CARSKEY BAY, KINTYRE (right).

BÀGH AN TIGH-STÒIR, CRAIGNISH, WITH SHUNA AND LUING BEYOND.

GARBH RÈISA AND THE SOUND OF JURA FROM CRAIGNISH POINT (left).

KILCHURN CASTLE (left) and LAG NA LUINGE, FRAOCH EILEAN AND EILEAN BEITH, LOCH AWE (above).
The placid inland waters of Loch Awe are a haven of peace today. But in medieval times the Campbells of Kilchurn,
the MacNaughtons of Fraoch Eilean ('Heather Island') and others fought out their bloody feuds here.

BALVICAR BAY, SEIL ISLAND.
An idyllic panorama in Argyll and the Isles: a seaweed-strewn shore, boats at anchor in a sheltered bay,
and rocky hills all around. Seil Island is known as one of the 'Slate Islands', which once had large quarries for roofing slate.

LOCH FYNE.

Loch Fyne extends 40 miles (65 km) inland from the Sound of Bute. Its cool seawaters are noted for their oysters.

INVERARAY CASTLE (left) and INVERARAY AND LOCH FYNE (above).

The castle and the distinctive whitewashed buildings of the burgh have served the Campbell Dukes of Argyll for over 500 years.

SCALPSIE BAY, ISLE OF BUTE.

COLINTRAIVE AND THE KYLES OF BUTE (right).

Southern Scotland, Glasgow and Edinburgh

The landscape of the south of Scotland contains a wealth of open country, forests, rivers and lochs, and its Southern Upland hills stretch from the North Channel to the North Sea through the Scottish borderlands. The hand of man is in evidence here too – in its battlefields spanning centuries of warfare with England, in ancient castles and abbeys, in monuments of industry – and most noticeably of all across the 'Central Belt' of Scotland, in the thriving international cities of Glasgow and Edinburgh.

DRUMLANRIG CASTLE, NITHSDALE, DUMFRIES AND GALLOWAY (left) and EDINBURGH CASTLE AND SKYLINE AT DUSK (above).

KELVINGROVE ART GALLERY AND MUSEUM, GLASGOW.

Glasgow is the largest city in Scotland and the third most populated in Britain. It is renowned for its impressive architectural heritage.

PARK CIRCUS AND PARK QUADRANT, KELVINGROVE, GLASGOW (left).

BURNS COTTAGE, ALLOWAY, SOUTH AYRSHIRE.

This 'auld clay biggin' was where Robert Burns, Scotland's national bard, was born on 25 January 1759.

THE ISLE OF ARRAN ACROSS THE SOUND OF BUTE.

Arran is sometimes described as 'Scotland in Miniature', as it is divided into highland and lowland areas by the Highland Boundary Fault.

CULZEAN CASTLE, SOUTH AYRSHIRE.

Robert Adam's impressive seat of the Kennedys stands amid Alexander Nasmyth's enchantingly designed gardens on the Ayrshire coast.

ST MARY'S LOCH FROM PENIESTONE KNOWE, SCOTTISH BORDERS.

St Mary's is the largest natural loch in the region and features on Britain's first official coast to coast walk, the Southen Upland Way.
The walk stretches 212 miles (340 km) across the Borders from Portpatrick on the Atlantic to Cockburnspath on the North Sea.

EVENING LIGHT IN THE SCOTTISH BORDERS.

Sweet pastures abound in the Border Country, sustaining cattle in the valleys and sheep on the hills.

CAERLAVEROCK CASTLE, NITHSDALE, DUMFRIES AND GALLOWAY.

These formidable red sandstone walls were home to the powerful Maxwells, lords of Nithsdale, for over 400 years.

HERMITAGE CASTLE, LIDDESDALE, SCOTTISH BORDERS.
The 'Black' Douglases's forbidding fortress guarded the road through Liddesdale, once 'the bloodiest valley in Britain'.

THE ETTRICK VALLEY, SCOTTISH BORDERS.

The Ettrick Valley was home to the self-taught Scottish poet and novelist James Hogg, who attained fame as the 'Ettrick Shepherd'.

THE BASS ROCK, FIRTH OF FORTH.

Scotland's Alcatraz during the notorious 'Killing Time' of the 1680s is now home to some 50,000 pairs of gannets.

ST ABB'S HEAD, SCOTTISH BORDERS (left).

MELROSE ABBEY, SCOTTISH BORDERS.

'SCOTT'S VIEW' – THE EILDON HILLS AND RIVER TWEED, SCOTTISH BORDERS.
Sir Walter Scott often rested at this, his favourite viewpoint. In the foreground lies the River Tweed and the ancient abbey
and chapel site of Old Melrose. The Eildon Hills (Roman, *Trimontium*, place of three mountains) rise in the distance.

BROUGHTON PLACE, SCOTTISH BORDERS.

Designed by Sir Basil Spence and completed in 1938, the white-harled residence seems perfectly at home in the landscape of the Border hills.

HUNDLESHOPE HEIGHTS, SCOTTISH BORDERS (right).

THE FORTH BRIDGE AND FIRTH OF FORTH.

The iconic cantilever bridge that crosses the Firth of Forth was one of the great engineering feats of the Victorian Age.
Over 55,000 tons of steel and 8 million rivets were used in its contruction. The final rivet, gold plated, was hammered in on March 4 1890.

EDINBURGH CASTLE AND CITY.

One of the world's most enchanting cities, Edinburgh began with its Castle over one thousand years ago. Today, Scotland's capital retains great character in the contrasting jumble of its medieval Old Town, and the elegant order of its Georgian New Town to the north.

Perthshire, Stirling and Fife

The counties of Perthshire, Stirling and Fife are where the Lowlands and Highlands meet, and their panoramas reflect this. The muted heather-carpeted mountain slopes along the west and north hint at the towering massifs that lurk beyond. The large inland lochs of placid water prepare the traveller for the long and often stormy sea lochs that cut deep into the western seaboard. The landscape to the south and east becomes more gentle. Here the fertile soils and the seas have combined to sustain a healthy population down the millennia.

LOCH LOMOND (left) and LOCH KATRINE AT DUSK (above), LOCH LOMOND AND THE TROSSACHS NATIONAL PARK.

BEN LOMOND & LOCH ARD, LOCH LOMOND AND THE TROSSACHS NATIONAL PARK.

BEN VENUE & LOCH KATRINE, LOCH LOMOND AND THE TROSSACHS NATIONAL PARK (left).

LOOKING NORTH-WEST ABOVE BEN MORE NEAR CRIANLARICH WITH BEN NEVIS IN THE DISTANCE.

INCHMAHOME, LAKE OF MENTEITH, LOCH LOMOND AND THE TROSSACHS NATIONAL PARK (right).

THE NATIONAL WALLACE MONUMENT, ABBEY CRAIG, STIRLING.

STIRLING CASTLE (left).

Stirling Castle has existed since at least 1110 AD, and was one of the main royal residences in medieval and early modern Scotland.

THE PASS OF KILLIECRANKIE, PERTHSHIRE.
The River Garry meandering through the pass looks peaceful in this winter scene, but a bloody battle took place here over 300 years ago that almost succeeded in returning the exiled Stuarts to the throne.

BLAIR CASTLE, PERTHSHIRE.

The original castle tower, built by John Comyn of Badenoch, dates from around 1269. This seat of the Dukes of Atholl nestles in Glen Garry, watched over by the heather-clad hills of the Forest of Atholl, where the imperious stag has been stalked for countless generations.

SCHIEHALLION, PERTHSHIRE.

BEN LAWERS ACROSS LOCH TAY, PERTHSHIRE (left).

CRAIL, FIFE.

This little port on the North Sea is perhaps the most picturesque of all the pleasant fishing villages dotted along the coast of the East Neuk of Fife. There is still fishing from the harbour here for crab and lobster, which are prized for their quality.

CELLARDYKE, ANSTRUTHER EASTER, FIFE.

ST ANDREWS, FIFE.

The attractive university town was the headquarters of the Scottish Church in medieval times, but its huge cathedral fell into ruins in the early 17th century. Today it is the 'home of golf', thanks to the challenging links courses (right) to the north-west of the city.

The Central Highlands and North-East Scotland

Stunning mountain scenery and stately castles take pride of place in the panoramas of the Central Highlands and North-East Scotland. The Cairngorms, Britain's most extensive mountain range, lie at the centre of the region. They are a paradise for wildlife, and contain many of the country's highest mountains. Down in the river valleys, and on the fertile agricultural plains beyond, impressive seats of medieval lordship grace the landscape. All along the North Sea coast lie little fishing villages and bustling market towns.

LOCH MALLACHIE, STRATHSPEY (left) and ROTHIEMURCHUS AND THE CAIRNGORMS (above), CAIRNGORMS NATIONAL PARK.

ST CYRUS, ANGUS.

GLAMIS CASTLE, ANGUS (left).

Home to the Earls of Strathmore, Glamis is associated with Macbeth, and was the birthplace of the late Queen Elizabeth the Queen Mother.

STONEHAVEN HARBOUR, ABERDEENSHIRE.

Pleasure craft now lounge around the harbour where a century and more ago hundreds of fishing
boats crammed in, as they followed the herring shoals heading south through the North Sea.

RRS *DISCOVERY* AND THE DISCOVERY CENTRE, DUNDEE.

Robert Falcon Scott's research ship set sail from Dundee in 1901 on his first epic journey into the unknown frontiers of Antarctica.

MONTROSE BASIN, ANGUS.
A broad tidal lagoon calms the waters of the River South Esk before channelling them into the North Sea.
Its 2530 acres (1024 ha) are a haven for wildfowl and wading birds.

CROVIE, ABERDEENSHIRE.
There are many distinctive fishing villages along the northern coast of Aberdeenshire with houses built gable-end onto the sea.

BENNACHIE, GARIOCH, ABERDEENSHIRE (right).
The slopes of Bennachie are thought to be where the battle of Mons Graupius was fought between the Caledonians and Romans in AD 83.

THE SANDS OF FORVIE AND THE RIVER YTHAN AT NEWBURGH, ABERDEENSHIRE.

The Forvie Sands are characteristic of the broad swathes of dunes that stretch along much of Aberdeenshire's east coast.

'QUEEN'S VIEW', CROMAR, ABERDEENSHIRE (left).

CASTLE FRASER, ABERDEENSHIRE.

Aberdeenshire is sometimes referred to as 'Castle Country', and the ancient seat of the Frasers is among the best.

FYVIE CASTLE, ABERDEENSHIRE (right).

BALMORAL CASTLE AND THE RIVER DEE, ROYAL DEESIDE, ABERDEENSHIRE.
Queen Victoria and Prince Albert were smitten with Balmoral, and in 1853 built their holiday retreat in
'this dear paradise' beside the River Dee. Royal Deeside remains dear to the royal family to this day.

GLEN CLUNIE NEAR BRAEMAR, ABERDEENSHIRE.

CORGARFF CASTLE, ABERDEENSHIRE (right).
The castle is now at peace, but in 1571 Lady Forbes and her entire household were burned to death therein.

THE CAIRNGORMS NATIONAL PARK.
The Cairngorms, pictured from the north (left) and from near Aviemore looking towards the Lairig Ghru (above), are the most extensive granite mountains in Scotland. They form the centrepiece of Britain's largest national park, established in 2003.

LOCH INSH, STRATHSPEY, CAIRNGORMS NATIONAL PARK.
Geese and whooper swans flock in wintertime to roost and feed in the marshes that lie to the south of the loch's placid waters.

SUNSET ACROSS STRATHSPEY AT ABERNETHY, CAIRNGORMS NATIONAL PARK (left).

COIRE AN T-SNEACHDA, NORTHERN CORRIES, CAIRNGORMS.

'The corrie of the snows' lies directly beneath the summit of Cairn Gorm. Whilst this mountain gives its name to the entire mountain range, and surrounding National Park, it bows in height to nearby Ben Macdui. The area is home to around a quarter of Britain's threatened flora and fauna.

AN GARBH COIRE, BEN MACDUI, SGOR AN LOCHAIN UAINE & CAIRN TOUL, CAIRNGORMS.

LOCH AN EILEIN, ROTHIEMURCHUS, CAIRNGORMS NATIONAL PARK.

CARRBRIDGE, STRATHSPEY, CAIRNGORMS NATIONAL PARK.
The old bridge over the River Dulnain was built for hearses heading for Duthil Kirk; hence its nickname 'Coffin Bridge'.

LOCH GARTEN, STRATHSPEY, CAIRNGORMS NATIONAL PARK.

STRATHSPEY FROM THE FOOTHILLS OF THE CAIRNGORM MOUNTAINS (right).

The Islands of Orkney and Shetland

The northern archipelagos of Orkney and Shetland present a very different panorama from the rest
of Scotland. Here, where the salt waters of the Atlantic Ocean and the North Sea meet, lie over 150 islands.
Some are sizeable and inhabited, most are little more than jagged rocks – skerries – isolated by the sea. High
ground is scarce. In its place a low, lush but largely treeless landscape predominates, one that has sustained
human life for well over 5,000 years, as its outstanding array of prehistoric monuments testify to.

HARRY'S PUND AND ESHA NESS, NORTHMAVINE, SHETLAND (left) and THE STONES OF STENNESS, MAINLAND, ORKNEY (above).

THE RING OF BRODGAR, MAINLAND, ORKNEY.

Originally comprised of 60 stones, the great ceremonial ring still contrives to overawe, just as it did in Neolithic times.

YESNABY, MAINLAND, ORKNEY (left).

BAY OF SKAILL, MAINLAND, ORKNEY.
Skaill Bay didn't exist when our Stone-Age forebears built Skara Brae (opposite). But the Atlantic's
relentless pounding eventually carved a way through the sandstone cliffs forcing the villagers to abandon their settlement.

142

SKARA BRAE PREHISTORIC VILLAGE, MAINLAND, ORKNEY.

The amazing little Stone-Age village beside the Bay of Skaill is around 5000 years old, and the best-preserved in northern Europe.

THE BERRY (above) and THE OLD MAN OF HOY (right), HOY, ORKNEY.

Hoy means 'high island' and the red sandstone cliffs and stacks along this Atlantic side reach as high as 1,140 feet (347m).

ST NINIAN'S TOMBOLO, SOUTH MAINLAND (left) and THE NOUP AND HELLABRICK'S WICK, FOULA (above), SHETLAND.

EAST BURRAFIRTH AND AITH VOE, MAINLAND, SHETLAND.

WICK OF SANDSAYRE AND WARD OF BURRALAND, SOUTH MAINLAND, SHETLAND.
Hardy sheep graze among the island's thin soils. Crofting is still a way of life for many Shetlanders.

MUCKLE FLUGGA LIGHTHOUSE AND OUT STACK FROM HERMA NESS, UNST, SHETLAND.
The tiny speck beyond the lighthouse, Out Stack, is the most northerly point of the British Isles.

ESHA NESS, NORTHMAVINE, SHETLAND.

MOUSA BROCH, MOUSA, SHETLAND.

Broch towers are unique to Scotland and may have served as fortified residences, or refuges. Mousa, at 43 ft (13 m) high,
is the most complete of all that remain. It was built over 2,000 years ago, probably by a local warlord.

GAADA STACK, FOULA, SHETLAND (right).

Foula is one of Britain's most remote inhabited islands. Located 20 miles west of Walls in Shetland, it's high cliffs and stacks teem with seabirds.

Northern Scotland

In Northern Scotland the overriding impression is of a remote and lonely landscape largely untouched
by the hand of man. Solitude is everywhere. It is there in the mountains of the North-West Highlands, which remain
aloof from each other rather than massed together as their fellows are further south. It is there on the white beach strands,
and atop the steep-cliffed headlands along the wild Atlantic coast. It is there too in the barren inland straths.
Only occasionally is that solitude broken, most notably in the city of Inverness, 'Capital of the Highlands'.

CAPE WRATH FROM FARAID HEAD, SUTHERLAND (left) and INVERPOLLY AND COIGACH, WESTER ROSS (above).

TRÀIGH ALLT CHÀILGEAG AND WHITEN HEAD, SUTHERLAND.

DORNOCH FIRTH AND BRIDGE WITH THE MOUNTAINS OF NORTH-WEST SUTHERLAND BEYOND (left).

This great firth is one of three that penetrates Northern Scotland's eastern seaboard. Dornoch Bridge was opened in 1991.

DUNNET BAY, CAITHNESS.
All along the north coast of Scotland, sandy beaches interplay with rocky headlands.
Dunnet Head to the east of Dunnet Bay (on the right) is the most northerly point on the British mainland.

STRATHY BAY, SUTHERLAND

BEN HOPE ACROSS LOCH HOPE, SUTHERLAND.

BEN LOYAL AND THE KYLE OF TONGUE, SUTHERLAND.

CRANSTACKIE, STRATH DIONARD AND FOINAVEN, SUTHERLAND.
Strath Dionard is a long glen flanked by the Foinaven ridge on the south-west, and Cranstackie to the north-east.
These ancient outposts in the extreme north-west Highlands remain wild and solitary and contain designated 'Special Areas of Conservation'.

SANDWOOD BAY, SUTHERLAND.

Remote Sandwood Bay is part of a large estate in the care of the John Muir Trust, which protects wild land for future generations.

OLDSHOREMORE WITH THE MOUNTAINS OF CRANSTACKIE, FOINAVEN AND ARKLE BEYOND, SUTHERLAND.

HANDA ISLAND ACROSS THE SOUND OF HANDA, SUTHERLAND (right).

SUILVEN, SUTHERLAND.

Suilven's unique 'sugarloaf' ridge is formed from 1000 million year old Torridonian sandstones overlaying older Lewisian gneiss, dating from 3000 million years ago. Its highest point, Caisteal Liath (Gaelic for grey castle), lies at the north-west end of the ridge.

LOCH ASSYNT, SUTHERLAND.

STAC POLLAIDH (STAC POLLY) AND LOCH LURGAINN, INVERPOLLY, WESTER ROSS.

LOCH KANAIRD AND COIGACH, WESTER ROSS.

Coigach's imposing headland noses into the Atlantic Ocean like some giant mammoth seeking cool waters.

THE SUMMER ISLES.

The clutch of little islands at the mouth of Loch Broom derive their name from their use as summer grazing.
They also found good use as anchorages during the herring-fishing boom in the 19th century.

ULLAPOOL, LOCH BROOM, WESTER ROSS.

This handsome seaport was founded as a 'new town' over 200 years ago to help Highlanders profit from the herring shoals.

LOCH DROMA, WESTER ROSS.

INVERNESS AND THE RIVER NESS (right).

The Western Isles

The Western Isles are also called the Outer Hebrides, and sometimes referred to as 'The Long Isle',
for the island chain is 130 miles (210 km) long and barely 30 miles (45 km) wide. The main island group includes
Lewis and Harris, North Uist, Benbecula, South Uist, and Barra. The islands are predominately low lying and covered in
peat bog, but they are fringed by outstanding sandy beaches. Remote St Kilda, a 'Dual World Heritage' site, lies some
40 miles (64 km) to the west of North Uist, and has the highest sea cliffs and stacks in the British Isles.

THE WEST COAST OF BARRA (left) and VALLAY STRAND, NORTH UIST (above).

TRÀIGH SCURRIVAL AND THE SOUND OF FUDAY, BARRA, WITH SOUTH UIST, ERISKAY AND FUDAY BEYOND.
The Isle of Barra lies towards the southern end of the Outer Hebridean chain of islands, and still sustains a large Gaelic-speaking population.

THE WILD FLOWERS OF THE MACHAIR (left).

KISIMUL CASTLE, CASTLE BAY, BARRA.
The seat of the chief of Clan MacNeil probably dates from the 15th century, and consists of a tower house and sturdy curtain wall.

SOUTH UIST AND BENBECULA ACROSS THE LITTLE MINCH (right).

LOCH DRUIDIBEG, SOUTH UIST.

Loch Druidibeg is a National Nature Reserve where opposites meet. Its western shores are graced by beaches and machair, while its eastern boundary rises to heather moorland. In-between lies a watery landscape of innumerable lochs, lochans and bog.

HECLA AND BEINN MHÒR ACROSS LOCH DRUIDIBEG, SOUTH UIST.

LOCH MADDY, NORTH UIST.

BEINN MHÒR AND BEINN BHREAC ACROSS LOCH MHIC PHÀIL, NORTH UIST.

Water predominates across North Uist, where half the landscape lies below sea level. The island is known for its rich birdlife, and the nature reserve at Balranald provides a safe haven for corncrakes, barnacle geese and corn buntings.

THE VILLAGE, ST KILDA.

The islands of St Kilda were occupied for some 4000 years, during which time the hardy St Kildans were self sufficient, relying on seabirds for food and fuel. After periods of illness and poverty the remaining 36 islanders were finally evacuated from the main island of Hirta in 1930.

OISEVAL AND DÙN FROM CONACHAIR, HIRTA (above) and BORERAY, STAC AN ARMIN AND STAC LEE (right), ST KILDA.
The enduring image of St Kilda is of stupefying cliffs rising from the Atlantic swell to 1,400 ft (427 m), and the commotion
of hundreds of thousands of seabirds – for Boreray is the home of the largest gannetry in the world.

186

TRÀIGH SEILEBOST (left) and TRÀIGH SCARASTA AND CHAIPAVAL (above), HARRIS.
Tràigh Seilebost and Tràigh Scarasta are two of the finest beaches (*tràigh* means 'beach') in the Western Isles, whilst on a clear day from the summit of Chaipaval, one can glimpse the remote archipelago of St Kilda way out in the Atlantic swell.

189

CALANAIS STANDING STONES, LEWIS.

These ancient standing stones may have been used to mark important astronomical events. Today, the monument stands in testament
to the timeless nature of Scotland's landscapes, and the people who have inhabited them throughout the ages.

Index of Places

First published in the U.K. in 2008 by Colin Baxter Photography Ltd, Grantown-on-Spey, PH26 3TA, Scotland. New edition 2014.
www.colinbaxter.co.uk
Photographs © Colin Baxter 2014.
Text by Chris Tabraham. Copyright © Colin Baxter Photography Ltd 2014.

ISBN 978-1-84107-412-2   Printed in China

Front cover: EILEAN DONAN CASTLE, West Highlands (top); LOCH GARTEN, Strathspey (bottom).   *Page one:* 'THE THREE SISTERS', Glencoe   *Back cover:* Eoligarry, BARRA, Western Isles